EMBRACE THE COMING LIGHT

*DAILY READINGS AND PRAYERS
FOR ADVENT*

EDDY EKMEKJI & TYLER WATSON

Embrace the Coming Light: Daily Readings and Prayers for Advent

Published by Eddy Ekmekji
Copyright © 2013 Eddy Ekmekji and Tyler Watson

"The deep darkness vanished into ordinary daylight, and the mystery of God was only made more splendid."

Marilynne Robinson, *Gilead*

DEDICATION

Eddy: To the good people of As You Are Church, who continue to shape my spirituality and love for God. Thank you for guiding me away from darkness and into the light.

Tyler: To my sisters and brothers of The Creek Covenant Church, who welcomed my family and fed us physically and spiritually, even when you hardly knew us. Thank you for letting your light shine in the darkness.

CONTENTS

WEEK 4
JOHN THE BAPTIST, MATTHEW 3.1–17

INTRODUCTION

In October of 2008, my (Tyler) wife and I spent a week camping in Yosemite Valley. We decided to hike to the top of Half Dome on our first full day in the park. Because the trek is seventeen miles round-trip, we started out very early. The Sun had not risen. Our small headlamps acted as our only sources of light. Even though the early stages of the trail were well-paved, we still walked slower than our normal pace, anxious that we might trip over some stray rock or step off an unseen ledge. It was cold. It was dark. We knew there were others making a similar trek, but we couldn't see them clearly. We might come around a corner and unintentionally scare a group of hikers. We felt alone.

As we journeyed, the daylight began to grow, little by little. Eventually we were able to see our path without artificial illumination. Our pace quickened and we turned off our headlamps. The darkness no longer shrouded our fellow hikers and we could enjoy conversations with them. We could now see the massive granite walls and trees that make Yosemite such a majestic place.

The darkness increased our anxiety, made us more vulnerable to danger, kept the landscape hidden from us, and isolated us from others. But the coming light of day chased away that darkness and brought us safety, beauty, and community.

Just as the light of the day illuminated our path and subdued our anxieties of hiking in the dark, Advent is a season of celebration for the Christian Church, in which we remember both how the ancient world (and our world) sat in darkness and how God gave us the light of Jesus Christ. Advent is a season of remembrance and hope.[1] During these four weeks, which mark the beginning of a new year in the Church, we celebrate the story of Jesus' birth and we look forward with hope to his eventual return, when he will fully establish his kingdom here on Earth.

---

[1] We derive the word advent from the Latin word, *adventus*, which means "coming."

The Jewish people of antiquity, our spiritual ancestors, saw the darkness in their world. They lived under the rule of the fierce Roman Empire. Many took this foreign occupation as a sign God had yet to return to Israel because of the sinfulness of the people.[2] They hoped and prayed for the Messiah to bring peace, freedom, and wholeness to Israel and ultimately, the world. The people of God sat in darkness, needing the light of a savior (Matthew 4.16). This darkness manifested itself in injustice and oppression. The people wallowed in isolation. They needed the light that would bring them freedom, wholeness, and community.

In the same way, we see the dark spaces in our world that need God's light. During Advent we not only joyfully commemorate God becoming human in Jesus millennia ago, we also pray with expectation, "Come again, Lord Jesus." During Advent we call out the suffering in our world and we pray for the light of God to chase away the darkness of sin, isolation, and injustice.

One of the season's great symbols, the Advent wreath, recreates the movement from darkness to light. We begin with the candles unlit, we are in darkness. Then each week, as we light one more candle, the space around the wreath becomes brighter. When we finally light the Christ candle on Christmas Eve, the wreath is fully aglow, its light enabling us to see clearly. Because of the light we can see the beauty around us. We can see God's presence. Light also creates community as it enables us to see each other.

Popular Western culture thinks of the four weeks leading to Christmas as little more than the biggest shopping season of the year. As followers of Jesus, we can easily lose sight of Advent and allow busyness and rampant consumerism to take our attention. We can mindlessly succumb to the season's sugar rush and ignore the real pain in this world as well as the real hope God gives. Fleming Rutledge beautifully describes why we need to stay in Advent and avoid rushing into Christmas: "Advent teaches us to delay Christmas in order to experience it truly when it finally comes. Advent is designed to show that the meaning of Christmas

---

[2] Thomas R. Hatina, "Exile," in *Dictionary of New Testament Background*, eds. Craig A. Evans and Stanley E. Porter (Downers Grove, IL: InterVarstiy Press, 2000), 348.

is diminished to the vanishing point if we are not willing to take a fearless inventory of the darkness."[3]

The to-do lists of the season take our focus away from the fact that Jesus is revealing himself to us. Our social media and other forms of technology facilitate our distraction and can ultimately isolate us from one another. We confound a tweet, status update, or text with actual community. Information broadcast in a status update cannot replace sharing a meal with a good friend. We will not notice God's surprising actions in our lives if we are too busy shopping or scrolling through our Pinterest boards. We therefore need practices that will remind us of the world-changing story of Jesus' incarnation. Jesus came to be with us in the midst of our pain and fraying relationships. He came to bring healing, not distractions. He came to free us from our selfishness. The quiet growing light of the Advent wreath contrasts the assaulting glitz of the season's commercials. We have to choose which light we will embrace during this season.

Embrace the Coming Light will lead you through the practices of reading, prayer, and other spiritual disciplines. Through these practices, you will immerse yourself in the story of Jesus' birth. You will follow the account in the Gospel of Matthew, focusing on four stories, one for each week of Advent. First you will read about Herod, the tyrannical puppet king of Judea whose greed and fear kept him isolated from God and others. In the second week, you will read about Joseph, Jesus' father, and his quiet faith, which remained open to surprises. In the third week you will read of the wise men, who traveled long distances to pay homage to Jesus, the newborn king of the Jews. In the fourth week, you will read about the fiery prophet, John the Baptist, who understood the radical and transformative meaning of God's kingdom inaugurated on Earth because of Jesus' presence and ministry. Readers will notice that none of the biblical figures in this guide are women. We acknowledge their missing stories. We have chosen to follow the Gospel of Matthew's birth narrative, which focuses on men. The Gospel of Luke gives prominence to women in its account of Jesus' birth.

You will read the Bible in a variety of ways, from a more analytical study to prayerful meditations. We ask questions to

---

[3] Fleming Rutledge, "Advent Begins in the Dark," in *The Bible and The New York Times* (Grand Rapids, MI: Eerdmans Publishing Company, 1998), 26.

prompt reflection and we recommend having a journal to record your insights and prayers. You will read voices of Christians throughout the centuries who meditated on the incarnation. Each week also includes a spiritual discipline that coincides with the character and theme of the week. The spiritual disciplines remind us life with God is not merely about learning ideas—though, learning the stories and traditions of the Christian faith is deeply important. Following Jesus affects every dimension of our lives, from how we spend our time to what we give our allegiance and worship.

Advent begins four Sundays before Christmas. It therefore is a different length each year, varying between 22 and 28 days, depending on when Christmas falls on the calendar. *Embrace the Coming Light* has 28 days of readings and prayers and can be used, with minor adjustments, in any year. We designed the readings and prayers in this guide for personal use, but there is no reason families or small groups cannot use them.

As you enter Advent, take time to reflect on your need and the world's need for Jesus to return and establish lasting peace and justice. May this stanza from the Advent hymn, "O Come, O Come Emmanuel," shape your imagination with its beautiful depiction of how God's growing light chases off darkness and isolation.

O come, Thou Dayspring, come and cheer
Our spirits by Thine advent here
Disperse the gloomy clouds of night
And death's dark shadows put to flight.
Rejoice! Rejoice!
Emmanuel shall come to thee, O Israel.

METHODS

In a recent visit to Sequoia National Park with my (Eddy) family for our annual summer vacation, we camped for five days and took in the majesty of the giant sequoias and the beautiful landscapes. One day, my eight-year-old and five-year-old climbed up the 400 steps to the summit of Moro Rock to take in a gorgeous view of the park's valleys.

Climbing the 800 foot-long stairway is quite a challenge to anyone, let alone children, yet we knew that once we finished the ascent, we would be rewarded with the satisfaction of having arrived to the top and the views below us. But for the children, there was a third incentive for the climb—they would get snacks at the summit.

Once we reached the top and took our obligatory family picture, the children found a spot to sit and enjoy the snacks I had promised them before we started the climb. While I took in the sights, my children focused on their snack and the desire to climb back down because they missed their mother. I was proud of the kids' feat and recognized my experience of climbing and arriving to the top was very different than theirs. They weren't as impressed by the views along the way nor were they all that impressed by the vista on top. They were mostly impressed by their accomplishment to get to the top and the snack they earned. While we shared a common purpose to climb the rock, we experienced the climb differently.

What I love about reading Scripture and engaging a relationship with God is that there is no one right way or method. Similarly, we may engage the Advent season and experience God devotionally through a variety of ways. We are uniquely created with particular desires and motivations. What may speak to my soul may be different than what engages my co-writer, Tyler. We have intentionally developed this devotional with varying methods of engaging the text to give us a broader experience of Advent. Our hope is that you gain a richer experience of God's word, and that would prepare you for the coming Christmas season.

The methods for this devotional will intersect between various Scripture studies and reflective exercises.

Each Sunday, we will begin a new week of engaging with one of the four characters from the Gospel of Matthew.

- On Sundays, we start with a devotional essay to introduce you to the character. We will also introduce a discipline for the week to help you create space for the Holy Spirit to deepen your understanding and reflections on Advent.
- On Mondays, you will study the passage as a Bible Study, where you will receive a set of questions for observation, interpretation, and application to help you understand the text.
- On Tuesdays, you will engage in an imaginative reading of the story. You will take on the character for the week and imagine the emotions and context at hand. In doing so, we hope you empathize with the character and see how God would speak to you in that place.
- On Wednesdays, you will read a psalm that overlaps with the themes of the week. This reading will give you another perspective of understanding the character and the theme.
- On Thursdays, you will experience *lectio divina*, an ancient method of reading Scripture slowly and paying attention to the one thought that God would have for you to focus on in this story.
- On Fridays, you will read a set of quotations from ancient and modern writers who have reflected on this character or theme.
- And on Saturdays, you will have a chance to reflect on the week to see how God has spoken to you through this character, the devotional, and the week's spiritual discipline. The Saturday reflections will be somewhat similar from week to week and are inspired by the Prayer of Examen developed by Ignatius of Loyola. The questions aim to help you pay attention to God's voice in your life.

We hope these diverse methods of engaging Scripture and the themes will give you a deeper love for God and a deeper understanding of how God is at work driving you from darkness and into the light during in this Advent season. Appreciating and understanding my children's posture toward Moro Rock gave me a richer appreciation for the landscape and the experience. We are confident that these methods will only enrich your love for God.

DISCIPLINES

During this Advent season and as part of the interaction with this handbook, we invite you to participate in a different spiritual discipline each week as a practical and tangible response to the devotionals of the week. Spiritual disciplines have been a part of the lives of believers and the Church since its inception in Acts 2.

Spiritual disciplines are not meant to distinguish us as more holy, more righteous, or more pious. Instead, they are tools that guide us toward recognizing the grace of God in us and around us as well as the insecurities and fears that have a hold on us. Adele Calhoun writes, "Spiritual disciplines give the Holy Spirit space to brood over our souls. Just as the Spirit hovered over the face of the deep at the dawn of creation, so he hovers over us today, birthing the ever-fresh Christ-life within."[4] When we embrace a spiritual discipline, we also embrace a posture of openness to God's transforming power over us.

At times, it can seem that a discipline feels challenging and at other times, it can feel fun. Neither of these feelings are the point of a spiritual discipline. The invitation to a discipline is not meant to be punitive, nor is it meant to enhance our pleasure. However we may feel about a discipline, the point of it is to lead us to be more open to the work of God in our lives.

The historic Church has embraced certain disciplines (such as prayer, celebration, fasting, solitude), and you will practice some of these as you follow this guide. At the same time, we do not have to be limited to these traditional disciplines. If the goal of a spiritual discipline is to give space for the Holy Spirit to brood, then disciplines can be formed and tailored in ways to serve someone's particular place in life or a community's particular needs.

A couple years ago, I (Eddy) had noticed that one of my staff's motives for ministry came out of a place of guilt. He never felt he was doing enough for others. Every moment of free time he had was riddled with fear and insecurity that he should be ministering

---

[4] Adele Ahlberg Calhoun, *Spiritual Disciplines Handbook: Practices that Transform Us* (Downers Grove, IL: IVP Books, 2005), 19.

to others. This young minister did not know how to truly rest and when he tried to rest from work, he felt guilty for resting. As I probed, I learned he loved to watch football but he could never enjoy a game because of his guilt. (Watching any football is three hours he could have spent doing more in ministry.) So for a season, I suggested he adopt a spiritual discipline of watching one game a week. I recognize this may seem odd as a spiritual discipline (especially since far too many Americans would probably abuse this discipline). And I would never recommend this as a rule across the board. But for this young minister, this discipline was what he needed—the freedom to watch a football game without guilt and to receive that as a gift from God.

This discipline was intended not so much as to give him pleasure, but to orient him toward learning and experiencing certain truths about God—God gives us rest and pleasure, we can be free from the demands of the ministry, and we can trust God for the work that is not yet done. For this season, the discipline seemed like a right way for him to embrace the brooding of the Holy Spirit.

In this Advent series, we invite you to embrace four disciplines that will create the space in your soul for the Holy Spirit to engage you on a deeper level as you journey from darkness and into the light of the Christmas celebration. We intend for each discipline to last a week, beginning on Sunday and ending the following Saturday. We will incorporate the disciplines of fasting from social media, solitude, generosity, and adoration. Each one of these disciplines is meant to create space for reflection on our spiritual deficits and space to embrace the work that God wants to do in our lives.

METHOD AND EXPLANATION OF THE DISCIPLINES

WEEK 1: FASTING FROM SOCIAL MEDIA

This week we challenge you to take a week-long hiatus from social media (Facebook, Twitter, Pinterest, and others). Social media can easily be a tool to fill a void of relationships in our lives. While these platforms can be a wonderful way of connecting and relating with others, they can also take the focus away from the immediate community God has for us.

By logging off of social media, we encourage you to fill that space with local relationships. Perhaps you want to call someone you haven't called in a while or meet a friend for dinner or a cup of coffee. And as much as possible, try to avoid texting in favor of more tangible forms of interaction. We lose the richness and gift of human contact when we cannot hear the voices of our friends and neighbors.

WEEK 2: SOLITUDE
Calhoun speaks of solitude as a way for us to "unmask the false self" and to "put ourselves in a place where God can reveal to us that we might not notice in the normal preoccupations of life."[5] For this discipline, we challenge you to create space in your week where you can spend some alone time—away from your phone, your distractions, your relationships, your work, etc. For some of you, you may only be able to commit an hour of solitude. For others of you, you may be able to go on a day-long personal retreat.

Regardless of what you are able to do, we encourage you to carve out space at some point in your week where you embrace quiet and alone space.

WEEK 3: GENEROSITY
Being generous with your time and money may already be a rhythm you carry, but this week, we invite you to intentionally practice generosity. The invitation to generosity is to express our charity for others as acts of worship for God. Generosity can take on many forms and should involve a mindful sacrifice on our part. Whatever path you take, remember to think of it not as a gesture of being nice but as a gesture of worshipping God. Consider taking someone out to lunch this week or volunteering at a local shelter. Perhaps you want to give an extra gift to a missionary or to your church.

WEEK 4: ADORATION
During this week, you will transition from the season of Advent and into the season of Christmas. This is the week we begin to celebrate the birth of Jesus, who is God in the flesh. As part of the

---

[5] Ibid., 113.

discipline of adoration, create space in your life to listen to worship music. Since we encourage you to keep a journal along with this devotional, take a day to write out a psalm of praise to celebrate God's goodness in your life. Finally, participate in a local worship service to honor and celebrate the birth of the king of the Jews.

WEEK 1

HEROD

MATTHEW 2.1–22

WEEK 1, SUNDAY, HEROD: WHEN AN INFANT FRIGHTENS A TYRANT

King Herod the Great may seem like a strange figure to reflect on during Advent. The man was, by any measure, a vicious tyrant.[6] He reached the throne and kept power through shrewd political machinations and killing his opponents. Once in power, the titular King of the Jews continued to imprison and execute those who questioned his authority. So long as he quelled revolts and paid taxes to Emperor Augustus, his Roman overlord, Herod had free reign to consolidate power however he wished. Challengers to his throne found themselves outmaneuvered and ultimately killed, including two of his own sons. Herod essentially bought the goodwill of the populace through cutting taxes at opportune times and building massive projects, most notably expanding the Temple in Jerusalem, making it one of the grandest buildings in the ancient world.

What does this cunning, ruthless, and violent tyrant have to show us about discipleship?

Near the end of his life, Herod looked to name his successor as King of the Jews. His family members jockeyed to become the heir to the throne. Over several years, Herod drafted six different wills, each time naming a different successor. Into this political powder keg, Matthew tells us foreign wise men (magi) appear, asking Herod where they can find the newborn King of the Jews. Imagine the shock Herod, the frighteningly insecure oppressor, must have felt when he heard of a possible new challenger to his throne.

Herod the Great's greed and lust for power certainly took him far from the Yahweh, the God of Israel. Yahweh desires political

---

[6] The historical information about Herod comes from Harold W. Hoener, "Herodian Dynasty," in *Dictionary of Jesus and the Gospels*, eds. Joel B. Green, Scot McKnight, and I. Howard Marshall (Downers Grove, IL: InterVarsity Press, 1992), 317-321.

leaders to maintain order through service, justice, and care for the poor, not through oppression and fear. At the same time, Herod understood if the King of the Jews had been born, his world would be radically changed. His time as tyrant would be over. He could not remain the same, but would have to submit to a different authority.

Does the reality of Jesus' birth radically reshape your life? Should it? Herod knew Jesus' birth meant his life would change. How has Jesus' incarnation changed your life?

Unfortunately Herod did not receive the announcement of the wise men as good news. He could have joined the wise men and worshipped the true King of the Jews. He could have stepped into the glorious light of God and received forgiveness, love, and peace. Instead he chose to remain in the darkness. He chose to isolate himself from God and others. Matthew tells us Herod responded to the news of Jesus' birth as he responded to all previous threats to his rule—he sought to kill the infant.

When you reflect on the reality of Jesus' birth, on the reality that the God of the universe became flesh and lived among us, how do you respond? Do you seek to align yourself more with God's purposes or do you resist it, like Herod?

This week will be difficult. You will look into the darkness of your sin and isolation. Social media allows us to drown out the voices of our pain. When we experience isolation we can log onto Facebook or text our friends and have a virtual interaction with others. For a moment we don't feel so alone. But such interaction is deceptive. This week you will fast from social media as you pray about the darkness in your life and in the world. Do not run from the pain, but go deep into it. Allow the pain you see to shape your prayers through the rest of Advent, when we remember Jesus' first coming and look with great hope for his return.

DISCIPLINE

Take some time today to plan for a week without social media. You may need to update your status and let people know that you are not available to connect via that medium. You may also want to plan how you will connect with people who text you since you are encouraged to fast from texting as well. Make a list of and initiate with people with whom you would like to talk, have a meal, visit, or have a phone conversation.

In the time of King Herod, after Jesus was born in Bethlehem of Judea, wise men from the East came to Jerusalem, [2] asking, "Where is the child who has been born king of the Jews? For we observed his star at its rising, and have come to pay him homage." [3] When King Herod heard this, he was frightened, and all Jerusalem with him; [4] and calling together all the chief priests and scribes of the people, he inquired of them where the Messiah was to be born. [5] They told him, "In Bethlehem of Judea; for so it has been written by the prophet:

[6] 'And you, Bethlehem, in the land of Judah,
are by no means least among the rulers of Judah;
for from you shall come a ruler
who is to shepherd my people Israel.' "

[7] Then Herod secretly called for the wise men and learned from them the exact time when the star had appeared. [8] Then he sent them to Bethlehem, saying, "Go and search diligently for the child; and when you have found him, bring me word so that I may also go and pay him homage." [9] When they had heard the king, they set out; and there, ahead of them, went the star that they had seen at its rising, until it stopped over the place where the child was. [10] When they saw that the star had stopped, they were overwhelmed with joy. [11] On entering the house, they saw the child with Mary his mother; and they knelt down and paid him homage. Then, opening their treasure chests, they offered him gifts of gold, frankincense, and myrrh. [12] And having been warned in a dream not to return to Herod, they left for their own country by another road.

[13] Now after they had left, an angel of the Lord appeared to Joseph in a dream and said, "Get up, take the child and his mother, and flee to Egypt, and remain there until I tell you; for Herod is about to search for the child, to destroy him." [14] Then Joseph got up, took the child and his mother by night, and went to Egypt, [15] and remained there until the death of Herod. This was to fulfill what had been spoken by the Lord through the prophet, "Out of Egypt I have called my son."

[16] When Herod saw that he had been tricked by the wise men, he was infuriated, and he sent and killed all the children in and around Bethlehem who were two years old or under, according to the time that he had learned from the wise men. [17] Then was fulfilled what had been spoken through the prophet Jeremiah:

[18] "A voice was heard in Ramah,
wailing and loud lamentation,
Rachel weeping for her children;
she refused to be consoled, because they are no more."

[19] When Herod died, an angel of the Lord suddenly appeared in a dream to Joseph in Egypt and said, [20] "Get up, take the child and his mother, and go to the land of Israel, for those who were seeking the child's life are dead." [21] Then Joseph got up, took the child and his mother, and went to the land of Israel. [22] But when he heard that Archelaus was ruling over Judea in place of his father Herod, he was afraid to go there. And after being warned in a dream, he went away to the district of Galilee. [23] There he made his home in a town called Nazareth, so that what had been spoken through the prophets might be fulfilled, "He will be called a Nazorean."

WEEK 1, MONDAY, BIBLE STUDY

READ MATTHEW 2.1–22

HISTORICAL BACKGROUND
King Herod, often referred to as "Herod the Great, King of the Jews," reigned from 40 BC to 4 BC in Judea. Appointed by his father (who himself was appointed by Caesar) as military prefect of the region, he eventually earned the title of "king of the Jews" (given to him by the Roman Senate) because of his impressive allegiance to the Romans and ruthless military rule.

Suspicious and highly paranoid of others, Herod systematically killed his enemies, including his wife and her family in fear that a revolt or coup would remove him from power.

During his reign, Herod extended Roman interests through various building and expansion projects. He had also rebuilt the temple in Jerusalem as a means of endearing himself to his subjects.

OBSERVATIONS
- Trace the various reactions King Herod has toward the birth of the Messiah.
- Compare Herod's response to the birth of the child to that of the wise men. What is similar? What is different?
- In what ways does Herod's presence and leadership affect outcomes in this story?

INTERPRETATION
- Why might Herod be frightened by the words and visit of the wise men?
- What would you say are Herod's fears and insecurities?
- In what ways does Herod act upon his fears?
- What could have been a better response from Herod upon hearing of the birth of the child?

APPLICATION
- How might insecurities dictate your decisions and relationships with others?
- What are some fears that have and can keep you from worshipping Jesus?
- Take a moment and be honest with yourself and God about the fears in your life that keep you from worshipping and knowing Jesus. As you confess those fears to God, ask God to give you courage in response to your insecurities.

WEEK 1, TUESDAY, IMAGINATIVE READING

READ MATTHEW 2.1–22 SLOWLY ONCE

Reflect on the following questions before reading the passage again.

- What kinds of pressures do you imagine King Herod is facing? He certainly feels the pressure of governing his own people and to do well in the eyes of the Roman authorities.
- How might the birth of the king of the Jews create insecurities for King Herod who is called the king of the Jews?
- In verse 3 we learn that King Herod is frightened. How might fear dictate action?

As you read the passage a second time, read it from the perspective of King Herod—an insecure and fearful monarch, who finds himself threatened by the rumors that a baby is born who can challenge his throne.

- How does the darkness you observe in King Herod expose the darkness in your inner life?
- What do you need from God when you find yourself in a place of insecurity and fear?

Spend some time in prayer, asking God to search your heart for those areas of darkness. In contrast to King Herod, ask God to give you promises and faith to overcome those fears and insecurities.

WEEK 1, WEDNESDAY, PSALM 6

We have chosen a psalm that coincides with the week's character and themes. The Psalms have been the prayer book of God's people throughout history. We mature in prayer by regularly spending time in the Psalms, which express the full arc of the human experience to God. Read through the psalm slowly, bringing to mind the story of Herod. Allow the words of the psalmist to become your own prayer.

PSALM 6

To the leader: with stringed instruments; according to The Sheminith. A Psalm of David.

1 O LORD, do not rebuke me in your anger,
    or discipline me in your wrath.
2 Be gracious to me, O LORD, for I am languishing;
    O Lord, heal me, for my bones are shaking with terror.
3 My soul also is struck with terror,
    while you, O Lord—how long?
4 Turn, O LORD, save my life;
    deliver me for the sake of your steadfast love.
5 For in death there is no remembrance of you;
    in Sheol who can give you praise?
6 I am weary with my moaning;
    every night I flood my bed with tears;
    I drench my couch with my weeping.
7 My eyes waste away because of grief;
    they grow weak because of all my foes.
8 Depart from me, all you workers of evil,
    for the Lord has heard the sound of my weeping.
9 The LORD has heard my supplication;
    the Lord accepts my prayer.
10 All my enemies shall be ashamed and struck with terror;
    they shall turn back, and in a moment be put to shame.

REFLECTION QUESTIONS

- Remember a time when you were frightened. What caused your fear and how did you respond?
- How does the psalmist's response to his fear compare to Herod's response to the news that troubles him? In what ways are you tempted to react like Herod when you are frightened?
- How might you use this psalm as a prayer to shape your response to frightful situations in the future?

WEEK 1, THURSDAY, *LECTIO DIVINA*

Find a place where you will not be distracted. Quiet yourself with some deep breaths. Pray for God—Father, Son, and Holy Spirit—to guide you through this reading.

LECTIO, "READING"

Read Matthew 2.1-22 again. Take your time. Do not focus on anything in particular.

Read the passage again. This time pay attention to a verse or couple of verses that stick out to you.

MEDITATIO, "MEDITATION"

Read that verse several times, slowly and gently.

Are you drawn to a specific word or phrase? Slowly chew on it. Take it in, that is, memorize it. Allow this word to interact with your concerns and desires. Pay attention to what thoughts and feelings this word stirs in you.

ORATIO, "PRAYER"

Ask God, "What are you saying to me through this word?" Listen. Let your meditations shape what you want to say to God.

CONTEMPLATIO, "CONTEMPLATION"

Rest in God's embrace. Let go of your words and be silent. Trust that Jesus fully and deeply loves you. Let the Holy Spirit minister to you.

Take a moment to reflect on your experience praying through this passage. If you use a journal, record your thoughts and prayers there.

WEEK 1, FRIDAY, WRITINGS

Each Friday in this guide, we include writings that further discuss the story and themes of the week. We invite you to ponder the wisdom of these voices that come to us through the centuries. Does something they write stir thoughts or emotions in you? Allow the words of these writers to shape your prayers today.

What does this mean, that it was in the time of a very malevolent king that God descended to earth, divinity entered into flesh, a heavenly union occurred with an earthly body? What does this mean? How could it happen that a tyrant could then be driven out by one who was not a king, who would free his people, renew the face of the earth and restore freedom? Herod, an apostate, had wrongly invaded the kingdom of the Jews, taken away their liberty, profaned their holy places, disrupted the established order, abolished whatever there was of discipline and religious worship. It was fitting therefore that God's own aid would come to succor that holy race without any human help. Rightly did God emancipate the race that no human hand could free. In just this way will Christ come again, to undo the antichrist, free the world, restore the original land of paradise, uphold the liberty of the world and take away all its slavery. — Peter Chrysologus, Sermons 156.5[7]

Christ is breaking open his way to you. He wants to again soften your heart, which has become hard. In these weeks of Advent while we are waiting for Christmas, he calls to us that he is coming and that he will rescue us from the prison of our existence, from fear, guilt, and loneliness.... Let us make no mistake about it. Redemption is drawing near. Only the question is: Will we let it come to us as well or will we resist it? Will we let ourselves be pulled into this movement coming down from heaven to earth or

---

[7] *Matthew 1–13, Ancient Christian Commentary on Scripture, New Testament* 1a, ed. Manlio Simonetti (Downers Grove, IL: InterVarsity Press, 2001), 21-22.

will we refuse to have anything to do with it? Either with us or without us, Christmas will come. It is up to each individual to decide what it will be. — Dietrich Bonhoeffer, *A Testament to Freedom*[8]

Humanity is born out of the necessity to exist. Christ, however, was not born out of the necessity of nature to exist but by his merciful will to save. He was appropriately born contrary to the law of human nature because he was beyond nature. Behold the strange and wonderful birth of Christ. It came through a line that included sinners, adulterers and Gentiles. But such a birth does not soil the honor of Christ. Rather, it commends his mercy.
— Anonymous[9]

---

[8] Dietrich Bonhoeffer, *A Testament to Freedom*, quoted in *A Year with Dietrich Bonhoeffer: Daily Meditations from His Letters, Writings, and Sermons*, ed. Carla Barnhill (San Francisco: HarperSanFrancisco, 2005), 384.

[9] *Matthew 1–13, Ancient Christian Commentary on Scripture, New Testament* 1a, 13.

WEEK 1, SATURDAY, REFLECTIONS

Take some time today to reflect on how God engaged with you through this devotional this week.

1. Where did you experience the presence of God this week?
2. How did the character of Herod expose the darkness in your life? How do you feel about that exposure?
3. How did the social media fast attune you to the work of God in your life?
4. What are your hopes and prayers for yourself, your community, and your world for this season?

WEEK 2

JOSEPH

MATTHEW 1.18–25, 2.13–15

WEEK 2, SUNDAY, JOSEPH: A FAITH OPEN TO SURPRISE

Joseph received news just as shocking as what Herod heard. The Gospel of Matthew makes it clear there was centuries-old prophetic hope for the advent of the Messiah, but only a few men would imagine it would be their fiancée who would be the virgin carrying God's anointed one. Like Herod, Joseph began in the dark. He was confused and afraid, but he addressed his fear in an entirely different manner than Herod. How Joseph responded to the good news offers us a beautiful example of discipleship.

The Gospel of Matthew describes Joseph as "a righteous man," that is, a man who upholds the teachings of the Torah.[10] Matthew uses this term to tell us Joseph was a person who was close to God, who knew God's heart, who allowed God's teaching to shape his character and reason. Matthew also implies that Joseph's plan to dismiss Mary quietly when he discovered she was pregnant with someone else's baby would have been the compassionate and godly thing to do under normal circumstances. Yet despite having God form his character, Joseph planned to do something that went against God's plan. How could that happen?

The news Joseph received could isolate him. Who would believe him if he said an angel visited him in a dream and told him that Mary was pregnant with God's child? Matthew does not say so, but it is easy to imagine Joseph's neighbors shunned him because he chose to stay engaged to Mary. Instead of allowing his fear drive him toward greed and violence like Herod did, Joseph trusted God, which transformed his isolation into solitude. There is an ancient Christian tradition of occasionally secluding ourselves from others with the intent of hearing God's voice. Through his solitude, we see Joseph learned to embrace the earliest community centered around Jesus: the holy family.

---

[10] Ben Witherington, III, "Birth of Jesus," in *Dictionary of Jesus and the Gospels*, 62.

What God did in the incarnation was so big, so radical, so surprising, even "a righteous man" like Joseph could not understand what was happening without God revealing the plan to him. Because God was up to something so far beyond anyone's imagination, even righteous people would be surprised. Joseph must embrace his solitude, where what was familiar was taken away, so that he might trust this new, surprising reality.

This story challenges common, but skewed views of spiritual formation and maturity. We may think with enough training, with enough shaping by God, we can reach a point in our lives in which we no longer need God's guidance—like the apprentice painter who studies and practices under her teacher for years, but eventually develops enough that she no longer needs the teacher and can create on her own. We might also accept the Western notion of maturity, in which the mature person is a self-sufficient, independent being who does not need others.

The Christian understandings of spiritual formation and maturity actually move in the opposite direction. As we grow in Christ, we understand and seek to foster a deeper dependency on God and community. We do want God to form our reasoning and characters, but in reading Joseph's story we see that no amount of reasoning and wisdom can take the place of prayer. We need to embrace solitude so that we can hear God afresh.

This week you will practice solitude, intentionally withdrawing from others so that you might experience God's new revelation. Before you do so, reflect on how God has surprised you recently. If you have not been surprised, ask to be surprised again in the practice of solitude. Joseph is a hero in this passage because as a person who was close to God's heart, he understood the God we read about in the Hebrew Bible was full of amazing surprises. To have a character shaped by God means we will not only act compassionately and justly, but we will also remain open to surprises.

DISCIPLINE

Take some time today to plan how you will intentionally withdraw from others and practice solitude. Take a look at your schedule and carve out that space where you will turn to solitude. In addition to the "when," where can you go to practice solitude? You may be able to be in solitude at home or you may need to spend that time at a retreat center, a library, or a park. Consider a place where you will be away from people—places like coffee shops will likely prevent you from experiencing God in solitude.

MATTHEW 1.18-25, 2.13-15

[18] Now the birth of Jesus the Messiah took place in this way. When his mother Mary had been engaged to Joseph, but before they lived together, she was found to be with child from the Holy Spirit. [19] Her husband Joseph, being a righteous man and unwilling to expose her to public disgrace, planned to dismiss her quietly. [20] But just when he had resolved to do this, an angel of the Lord appeared to him in a dream and said, "Joseph, son of David, do not be afraid to take Mary as your wife, for the child conceived in her is from the Holy Spirit. [21] She will bear a son, and you are to name him Jesus, for he will save his people from their sins." [22] All this took place to fulfill what had been spoken by the Lord through the prophet:

[23] "Look, the virgin shall conceive and bear a son,
and they shall name him Emmanuel,"

which means, "God is with us." [24] When Joseph awoke from sleep, he did as the angel of the Lord commanded him; he took her as his wife, [25] but had no marital relations with her until she had borne a son; and he named him Jesus.

MATTHEW 2

[13] Now after they had left, an angel of the Lord appeared to Joseph in a dream and said, "Get up, take the child and his mother, and flee to Egypt, and remain there until I tell you; for Herod is about to search for the child, to destroy him." [14] Then Joseph got up, took the child and his mother by night, and went to Egypt, [15] and remained there until the death of Herod. This was to fulfill what had been spoken by the Lord through the prophet, "Out of Egypt I have called my son."

WEEK 2, MONDAY, BIBLE STUDY

READ MATTHEW 1.18–25, 2.13–15

HISTORICAL BACKGROUND

Marriage in the Biblical world is generally defined as "a state in which a man and woman can live together in sexual relationship with the approval of their social group."[11] In this passage we read that Joseph and Mary were engaged but we also see the author calling Joseph "her husband." The ancient communities often regarded betrothals almost as binding as marriage itself. Dissolving a betrothal would have been no private matter and would have brought much shameful attention to Mary.

OBSERVATIONS

- How does the author describe Joseph?
- What do the angel's words to Joseph reveal to the reader about Joseph's heart and posture?
- What are the various ways Joseph advocates for others in this passage?
- What challenges does Joseph face in the story?

INTERPRETATION

- Why might the author's descriptions of Joseph be important to the outcome of the story?
- How does Joseph respond to the various challenges he faces?
- What roles do dreams play in Joseph's life? Why might God use dreams to speak to Joseph?
- Why is it important for Joseph to know the identity of the child? How does that knowledge affect his faith?
- How did Joseph risk his reputation to stand with Mary?

---

[11] J. S. Wright and J. A. Thompson, "Marriage," in *New Bible Dictionary* 3rd ed., eds. D. R. W. Wood, I. H. Marshall, A. R. Millard, J. I. Packer, and D. J. Wiseman, (Downers Grove, IL: InterVarsity Press, 1996), 732.

APPLICATION

- Where are the areas of your life (work, school, home) where it may be unpopular to exercise faith? How may the fear of the backlash keep you from faithfulness?
- How does it feel to potentially risk your reputation to stand with those who (like Mary) may have been outcasts?
- What truths do you need to know about Jesus? How may those truths give you courage in the challenges you face?
- Make a list of praises and characteristics you appreciate about Jesus. How might these truths empower your faith?

WEEK 2, TUESDAY, IMAGINATIVE READING

READ MATTHEW 1.18–25, 2.13–15 SLOWLY ONCE

Reflect on the following questions before reading the passage again.

- What kinds of repercussions will Joseph, a righteous man, face if he goes through with this marriage? What kinds of repercussions will he face if he dissolves the engagement?
- What must it be like for Joseph to interact with the angel in the dream?
- What does courage look like for Joseph?

As you read the passage a second time, read it from the perspective of Joseph who commits to Mary despite the scandal taking place in his own community.

- How does Joseph's courage address areas of fear and insecurities in your own life?
- Has God intervened in your life to speak courage against the fears you feel? If he hasn't, what do you need from God to walk in courage and faith?

Spend some time in prayer, asking God to give you boldness and courage. List the areas of fear that are guiding your decision and ask God to speak words of truth and courage into those dark areas.

WEEK 2, WEDNESDAY, PSALM 8

We have chosen a psalm that coincides with the week's character and themes. The Psalms have been the prayer book of God's people throughout history. We mature in prayer by regularly spending time in the Psalms, which express the full arc of the human experience to God. Read through the psalm slowly, bringing to mind the story of Herod. Allow the words of the psalmist to become your own prayer.

PSALM 8

To the leader: according to The Gittith. A Psalm of David.

1   O LORD, our Sovereign,
    how majestic is your name in all the earth!
  You have set your glory above the heavens.
2   Out of the mouths of babes and infants
  you have founded a bulwark because of your foes,
    to silence the enemy and the avenger.
3   When I look at your heavens, the work of your fingers,
    the moon and the stars that you have established;
4   what are human beings that you are mindful of them,
    mortals that you care for them?
5   Yet you have made them a little lower than God,
    and crowned them with glory and honor.
6   You have given them dominion over the works of your
      hands;
    you have put all things under their feet,
7   all sheep and oxen,
    and also the beasts of the field,
8   the birds of the air, and the fish of the sea,
    whatever passes along the paths of the seas.
9   O LORD, our Sovereign,
    how majestic is your name in all the earth!

REFLECTION QUESTIONS
- The psalmist beautifully expresses awe and surprise at God's great works. When was the last time God overwhelmed you with awe and wonder?
- How has the practice of solitude opened your eyes to God's works? How do you want to respond to God?
- How might you foster surprise on a regular basis?

WEEK 2, THURSDAY, *LECTIO DIVINA*

Find a place where you will not be distracted. Quiet yourself with some deep breaths. Pray for God—Father, Son, and Holy Spirit—to guide you through this reading.

LECTIO, "READING"

Read 1.18-25, 2.13-15 again. Take your time. Do not focus on anything in particular.

Read the passage again. This time pay attention to a verse or couple of verses that stick out to you.

MEDITATIO, "MEDITATION"

Read that verse several times, slowly and gently.

Are you drawn to a specific word or phrase? Slowly chew on it. Take it in, that is, memorize it. Allow this word to interact with your concerns and desires. Pay attention to what thoughts and feelings this word stirs in you.

ORATIO, "PRAYER"

Ask God, "What are you saying to me through this word?" Listen. Let your meditations shape what you want to say to God.

CONTEMPLATIO, "CONTEMPLATION"

Rest in God's embrace. Let go of your words and be silent. Trust that Jesus fully and deeply loves you. Let the Holy Spirit minister to you.

Take a moment to reflect on your experience praying through this passage. If you use a journal, record your thoughts and prayers there.

WEEK 2, FRIDAY, WRITINGS

Each Friday in this guide, we include writings that further discuss the story and themes of the week. We invite you to ponder the wisdom of these voices that come to us through the centuries. Does something they write stir thoughts or emotions in you? Allow the words of these writers to shape your prayers today.

I would say about individuals, an individual dies when he ceases to be surprised. I am surprised every morning that I see the sunshine again. When I see an act of evil, I'm not accommodated. I don't accommodate myself to the violence that goes on everywhere; I'm still surprised. That's why I'm against it, why I can hope against it. We must learn how to be surprised. Not to adjust ourselves. I am the most maladjusted person in society. — Abraham Joshua Heschel[12]

Joseph was so free from the passion of jealousy as to be unwilling to cause distress to the Virgin, even in the slightest way. To keep Mary in his house appeared to be a transgression of the law, but to expose and bring her to trial would cause him to deliver her to die. He would do nothing of the sort. So Joseph determined to conduct himself now by a higher rule than the law. For now that grace was appearing, it would be fitting that many tokens of that exalted citizenship be expressed. It is like the sun not yet arisen, but from afar more than half the world is already illumined by its light. So did Christ, when about to rise from that womb—even before his birth—cast light upon all the world. — John Chrysostom, The Gospel of Matthew, Homily 4.4.[13]

---

[12] "The Spiritual Audacity of Abraham Joshua Heschel," *On Being,* December 6, 2012, http://www.onbeing.org/program/spiritual-audacity-abraham-joshua-heschel/transcript/4951#main_content, accessed October 24, 2013.

[13] *Matthew 1-13, Ancient Christian Commentary on Scripture,* ed. Manilo Simonetti, 14-15.

The Desert Fathers did not think of solitude as being alone, but as being alone with God. They did not think of silence as not speaking, but as listening to God. Solitude and silence are the context within which prayer is practiced. — Henri Nouwen, *The Way of the Heart*[14]

It is this hiddenness that gives Advent its special character. The church's life in Advent is hidden with Christ until he comes again, which explains why so much of what we do in this night appears to be failure, just as his life appeared to end in failure. If Jesus is the Son of God, he is also the One who identifies himself with 'the least, the last, and the lost,' who takes their part, who is born into the world as a member of the lowest class on the social ladder and does not cease to identify himself with our human fate until he is given up to die the death of a slave. This is not the end of the story. It is the beginning of the end.... In a very deep sense, the entire Christian life in this world is lived in Advent, between the first and second comings of the Lord, in the midst of the tension between things the way they are and the things the way they ought to be.
— Fleming Rutledge, "Advent Begins in the Dark"[15]

---

[14] Henri J.M. Nouwen, *The Way of the Heart: The Spirituality of the Desert Fathers and Mothers* (New York: HarperCollins, 1981), 69.
[15] Fleming Rutledge, "Advent Begins in the Dark," in *The Bible and The New York Times* (Grand Rapids, MI: Eerdmans Publishing Company, 1998), 29.

WEEK 2, SATURDAY, REFLECTIONS

Take some time today to reflect on how God engaged with you through this devotional this week.

1. Where did you experience the presence of God this week?
2. Like Joseph, how were you surprised by God's work and presence in your life this week?
3. How did the discipline of solitude attune you to the work of God in your life?
4. What are your hopes and prayers for yourself, your community, and your world for the season?

WEEK 3

THE WISE MEN

MATTHEW 2.1–12

WEEK 3, SUNDAY, THE WISE MEN: DON'T MISS THE INVITATION

There rarely is a telling of the birth story of Jesus without a mention of these wise men, or magi. They take up a short amount of space and the story of these wise men is told in the same narrative as King Herod. We know little about these men and never hear of them again, yet they are the first worshippers of the Messiah according to the Gospel of Matthew.

We know that they were not Jewish and came from the East (probably Persia). They were astrologers of some sort, since the observations of the cosmos is what led them to Jesus. And we can infer that they came from some wealth as expressed in their lavish gifts of gold, frankincense, and myrrh.

While they knew little about Jesus, what they knew was enough to propel them on a journey of discovery and worship. Their search for God began with God's intervention. Through the sign of the star—which presumably all saw but few interpreted—God spoke to these men through the things that made most sense to them.

Do we have the discernment and reflective discipline to pause and observe the ways that God uses the things in our lives to lead us to worship? Not unlike the ancient peoples, few of us may notice the ways that God is inviting us to worship and know him.

The Advent season is also known as the busiest shopping season of the year. And perhaps like those ancients, we can miss the invitations from God to worship Jesus and to embrace the good news that he has come and dwelt among us. God spoke to those men through the things that made most sense to them— perhaps it is in the busyness and familiarity of this season where God is speaking to you.

Once they found Jesus, the wise men honored and worshipped him with lavish gifts. Their generosity stood in contrast to Herod. While the wise men focused their worship on Jesus, Herod focused his worship on his own insecurities, fears, and lust for power. Advent challenges us to be generous people. And the true generosity of the wise men stands in contrast with the false generosity that we can see in the culture around us.

The holiday season seems to press us to be more about Christmas wish lists and anxiety-driven generosity. Will they like our gifts? Will I find the best deal? What am I going to get them for Christmas? The long lines at the return counter of retail stores illustrates this false generosity where generosity is commoditized and people feel free to return gifts to buy what they want.

This is not the generosity exhibited by the wise men who gave as an act of worship. This week you will be challenged to honor and praise God with generosity. As you are generous with others, consider this as your worship to Jesus, who taught us in Matthew 25.40 that extending generosity toward another is extending generosity toward Jesus.

Generosity is an act of worship. We do not give for the sake of giving but because we respond to the invitation to honor and praise God with our gifts. Jesus did not need the gifts of the wise men. Generosity is primarily an expression of our faith. We can be generous because we know a generous God. Generosity is a response to God who is far more generous with us. As you practice generosity this week, pay attention to the ways that God has been generous toward you, whether it is through his provisions, his healing presence and power, the gift of community, the joy of rest, or the invitations to minister to others.

DISCIPLINE
Take some time and identify how you will practice generosity this week. While the intention of this discipline is to press you to be generous with your finances, you may find that God is inviting you to be generous with your time or your possessions. Second, with whom can you be generous? Remember that this is not so much about caring for a need or boosting our own egos, but about expressing our worship.

MATTHEW 2:1-12

In the time of King Herod, after Jesus was born in Bethlehem of Judea, wise men from the East came to Jerusalem, ² asking, "Where is the child who has been born king of the Jews? For we observed his star at its rising, and have come to pay him homage." ³ When King Herod heard this, he was frightened, and all Jerusalem with him; ⁴ and calling together all the chief priests and scribes of the people, he inquired of them where the Messiah was to be born. ⁵ They told him, "In Bethlehem of Judea; for so it has been written by the prophet:

⁶   'And you, Bethlehem, in the land of Judah,
    are by no means least among the rulers of Judah;
    for from you shall come a ruler
    who is to shepherd my people Israel.' "

⁷ Then Herod secretly called for the wise men and learned from them the exact time when the star had appeared. ⁸ Then he sent them to Bethlehem, saying, "Go and search diligently for the child; and when you have found him, bring me word so that I may also go and pay him homage." ⁹ When they had heard the king, they set out; and there, ahead of them, went the star that they had seen at its rising, until it stopped over the place where the child was. ¹⁰ When they saw that the star had stopped, they were overwhelmed with joy. ¹¹ On entering the house, they saw the child with Mary his mother; and they knelt down and paid him homage. Then, opening their treasure chests, they offered him gifts of gold, frankincense, and myrrh. ¹² And having been warned in a dream not to return to Herod, they left for their own country by another road.

WEEK 3, MONDAY, BIBLE STUDY

READ MATTHEW 2:1–12

HISTORICAL BACKGROUND

Magi, or wise men, were non-Jewish (generally thought to be Persian) religious leaders and astrologers. They may have had some sort of priestly function.

Frankincense is an expensive spice and extremely odoriferous. It was an ingredient in the holy anointing oil and was burnt with various other offerings as part of the cereal offering. Myrrh was also a fragrance used in the holy anointing oil. It was also used as part of the burial preparation process.[16]

OBSERVATIONS
- What do the wise men know about this child?
- In what ways did the wise men learn about the birth of Jesus?
- What does the writer tell us is the purpose of their search for Jesus?

INTERPRETATION
- Why might the wise men be interested in paying homage to Jesus?
- Why might astrological phenomena play a role in the story?
- What do the gifts of the wise men reveal about them? What do they reveal about Jesus?
- Trace how the wise men's understanding of child progressed in this story.

---

[16] F. N. Hepper. "Herbs and Spices," in *New Bible Dictionary* 3rd ed., 466.

APPLICATION

- In what ways does God generally get your attention to orient you toward worshipping him?
- How may God invite you to be generous in your worship? How might your knowledge about Jesus affect your worship of him?
- Take stock of how you steward your material possessions. Does your relationship with "stuff" reflect your faith and worship of Jesus?

WEEK 3, TUESDAY, IMAGINATIVE READING

READ MATTHEW 2.1–12 SLOWLY ONCE

Reflect on the following questions before reading the passage again.

- What emotions guide the wise men in their search for the child?
- The journey presumably took weeks if not months. What sustains their spirits during that journey?
- How would you describe the character of these men?

As you read the passage a second time, read it from the perspective of the wise men—a tribe of educated and devout men who were not of the Jewish faith but who were certainly faithful to seek the child Jesus.

- How do you relate to the emotions of searching for Jesus?
- These wise men have at least one detour on their way to Bethlehem, but that does not keep them from searching. How do detours and roadblocks in your life inform your spirituality and relationship with God?
- What kind of character that you see in these men do you hope to see in yourself?

Spend some time in prayer, asking God to give you the perseverance and joy to pursue Jesus.

WEEK 3, WEDNESDAY, PSALM 19

We have chosen a psalm that coincides with the week's character and themes. The Psalms have been the prayer book of God's people throughout history. We mature in prayer by regularly spending time in the Psalms, which express the full arc of the human experience to God. Read through the psalm slowly, bringing to mind the story of Herod. Allow the words of the psalmist to become your own prayer.

PSALM 19

To the leader. A Psalm of David.

1 The heavens are telling the glory of God;
   and the firmament proclaims his handiwork.
2 Day to day pours forth speech,
   and night to night declares knowledge.
3 There is no speech, nor are there words;
   their voice is not heard;
4 yet their voice goes out through all the earth,
   and their words to the end of the world.
   In the heavens he has set a tent for the sun,
5 which comes out like a bridegroom from his wedding
      canopy,
   and like a strong man runs its course with joy.
6 Its rising is from the end of the heavens,
   and its circuit to the end of them;
   and nothing is hid from its heat.
7 The law of the LORD is perfect,
   reviving the soul;
   the decrees of the LORD are sure,
   making wise the simple;
8 the precepts of the LORD are right,
   rejoicing the heart;
   the commandment of the LORD is clear,
   enlightening the eyes;

9 the fear of the LORD is pure,
      enduring forever;
   the ordinances of the LORD are true
      and righteous altogether.
10 More to be desired are they than gold,
      even much fine gold;
   sweeter also than honey,
      and drippings of the honeycomb.
11 Moreover by them is your servant warned;
      in keeping them there is great reward.
12 But who can detect their errors?
      Clear me from hidden faults.
13 Keep back your servant also from the insolent;
      do not let them have dominion over me.
   Then I shall be blameless,
      and innocent of great transgression.
14 Let the words of my mouth and the meditation of my heart
      be acceptable to you,
      O LORD, my rock and my redeemer.

REFLECTION QUESTIONS
- Like the wise men, the writer of this psalm finds God's revelation in creation. This revelation draws the psalmist to reflect on how God also gives revelation in Scripture.
- How have you seen God's revelation in creation? In what other ways have you experienced divine revelation?
- How has receiving this news from God shaped your life? Offer a prayer like the psalmist, who wishes his thoughts and meditations will be acceptable to God.

WEEK 3, THURSDAY, *LECTIO DIVINA*

Find a place where you will not be distracted. Quiet yourself with some deep breaths. Pray for God—Father, Son, and Holy Spirit—to guide you through this reading.

LECTIO, "READING"

Read Matthew 2.1-12 again. Take your time. Do not focus on anything in particular.

Read the passage again. This time pay attention to a verse or couple of verses that stick out to you.

MEDITATIO, "MEDITATION"

Read that verse several times, slowly and gently.

Are you drawn to a specific word or phrase? Slowly chew on it. Take it in, that is, memorize it. Allow this word to interact with your concerns and desires. Pay attention to what thoughts and feelings this word stirs in you.

ORATIO, "PRAYER"

Ask God, "What are you saying to me through this word?" Listen. Let your meditations shape what you want to say to God.

CONTEMPLATIO, "CONTEMPLATION"

Rest in God's embrace. Let go of your words and be silent. Trust that Jesus fully and deeply loves you. Let the Holy Spirit minister to you.

Take a moment to reflect on your experience praying through this passage. If you use a journal, record your thoughts and prayers there.

WEEK 3, FRIDAY, WRITINGS

Each Friday in this guide, we include writings that further discuss the story and themes of the week. We invite you to ponder the wisdom of these voices that come to us through the centuries. Does something they write stir thoughts or emotions in you? Allow the words of these writers to shape your prayers today.

To be a Christian is, yes, to live in solidarity every day of our lives with those who sit in darkness and in the shadow of death, but also to live most truly in the unshakeable hope of those who expect the dawn. — Fleming Rutledge, "Advent Begins in the Dark"[17]

One day, at the last judgment, he will separate the sheep and the goats and will say to those on his right: "Come, you blessed,.... I was hungry and you fed me...." (Matt. 25:34ff). To the astonished question of when and where, he answered: "What you did to the least of these, you have done to me...." (Matt. 25:40). With that we are faced with the shocking reality: Jesus stands at the door and knocks, in complete reality. He asks you for help in the form of a beggar, in the form of a ruined human being in torn clothing. He confronts you in every person that you meet. Christ walks on the earth as your neighbor as long as there are people. He walks on the earth as the one through whom God calls you, speaks to you, and makes his demands. That is the greatest seriousness and the greatest blessedness of the Advent message. Christ stands at the door. He lives in the form of the person in our midst. Will you keep the door locked or open it to him? — Dietterich Bonhoeffer, *A Testament to Freedom*[18]

At times we may feel that we do not need God, but on the day when the storms of disappointment rage, the winds of disaster

---

[17] Rutledge, "Advent Begins in the Dark," in *The Bible and The New York Times*, 30.
[18] Bonhoeffer, *A Testament to Freedom*, quoted in *A Year with Dietrich Bonhoeffer: Daily Meditations from His Letters, Writings, and Sermons*, 382.

blow, and the tidal waves of grief beat against our lives, if we do not have a deep and patient faith our emotional lives will be ripped to shreds. There is so much frustration in the world because we have relied on gods rather than God. We have genuflected before the god of science only to find that it has given us the atomic bomb, producing fears and anxieties that science can never mitigate. We have worshiped the god of pleasure only to discover that thrills play out and sensations are short-lived. We have bowed before the god of money only to learn that there are such things as love and friendship that money cannot buy and that in a world of possible depressions, stock market crashes, and bad business investments, money is a rather uncertain deity. These transitory gods are not able to save us or bring happiness to the human heart. Only God is able. It is faith in him we must rediscover. With this faith we can transform bleak and desolate valleys into sunlit paths of joy and bring new light into dark caverns of pessimism. — Martin Luther King, Jr., "Our God is Able"[19]

---

[19] Martin Luther King, Jr., "Our God is Able," in *Strength to Love* (Philadelphia: Fortress Press, 1963), 112-113.

WEEK 3, SATURDAY, REFLECTIONS

Take some time today to reflect on how God engaged with you through this devotional this week.

1. Where did you experience the presence of God this week?
2. Like the wise men, how did God speak to you through your surroundings or some of the familiar routines of this season?
3. How did the discipline of generosity attune you to the work of God in your life?
4. What are your hopes and prayers for yourself, your community, and your world for the season?

WEEK 4

JOHN THE BAPTIST

MATTHEW 3.1–17

WEEK 4, SUNDAY, JOHN THE BAPTIST: A WILD PROPHET EMBRACES THE COMING LIGHT

John the Baptist seems to come onto the scene in the Gospel narrative with little warning. His appearance is atypical, his ministry is on the margins of society (in the wilderness), his message is full of judgment, and his method (baptisms) seems suspect—Jews didn't usually get baptized.[20]

The Gospel of Matthew gives us very little background to John. We know from other accounts that he was related to Jesus, but that does not seem to be of any interest to the writer. John's ministry of baptism and preparation culminated in him baptizing Jesus, which launched Jesus' public ministry.

In Matthew 3, John's ministry is interpreted through Isaiah 40 where a prophetic voice prepares the ministry and revelation of the Messiah. How did John prepare for Jesus? By hearing people's confessions and baptizing them. And people came to John by the droves. While the modern reader may question the effectiveness of John's methods, the text suggests that people joyfully received John's message and ministry.

The transformation that took place in the wilderness would prepare people for the message and ministry of Jesus. No one knew that better than John. John knew the true identity of Jesus and could not bring himself to baptize him. How could he baptize the one whom he had declared to be more powerful than he? How could he baptize with water the one who would baptize with the Holy Spirit and fire?

---

[20] "Like many other ancient peoples, Jewish people practiced ceremonial washings. Their only once-for-all ceremonial washing, however, was the immersion that non-Jews had to go through when they converted to Judaism. Non-Jews who were converting to Judaism would immerse themselves in water, probably under the supervision of a religious expert. John's baptizing activity fits this model." Craig S. Keener, *The IVP Bible Background Commentary: New Testament* (Downers Grove, IL: InterVarsity Press, 1993), Mark 1:4-5, electronic edition.

By knowing the true identity of Jesus, John could fully worship the Messiah. Of all the characters we have studied in this Advent series, John was most aware of the identity and worth of Jesus. He knew that Jesus was the Messiah. His ministry was devoted to prepare the way of the Christ and when he interacted with Jesus at the banks of the Jordan River, he submitted to Jesus' leadership as he hesitated to baptize him along with the crowds.

John's ministry of preparation was an invitation for people to recognize the darkness of sin within them and to embrace the freedom and grace of the Messiah. Celebrating Christmas is to accept truth about our darkness and truth about the saving grace of the Messiah.

Confession of sin and walking in repentance are expressions of a transformed person who trusts in God's forgiveness and goodness. The people who went to John to be baptized recognized that the life John invited them into was far superior to the life they had known. The confession of sin and the act of baptism are part of the transformation process to publically and personally declare we want to be defined by the ways of God and not the ways of our sins.

John seemed to reserve harsh words for the religious elite (Sadducees and Pharisees) as he called them "a brood of vipers" and pronounced judgment on their posture toward the spiritual life. What is striking about John was that he recognized the dangers of living in darkness (even for religious folks).

His call to the religious people is his call to all people—to expose the darkness in our lives so that we can embrace the light of Jesus. The Messiah coming to live among us is offensive to the darkness in ourselves. The Incarnation is a threat to the status quo, even the status quo of our lives.

Advent leads us to a celebration of the birth of Jesus. We can truly adore and celebrate Christmas when we renounce the shame and power of darkness and embrace Jesus.

In this final week of Advent, you are invited into the discipline of adoration. As we transition from Advent to Christmas, we celebrate and worship the God who became flesh. Practicing adoration is not just singing Christmas songs and exchanging gifts on Christmas day, it's choosing to be a transformed people who joyfully confess our sins, embrace repentance, and turn our posture toward worshipping Jesus.

DISCIPLINE
Take some time today to plan how you will celebrate the incarnation and the season of Christmas. You may have a number of traditions that help you celebrate. Do you need to make any changes to those traditions to help you with the discipline of adoration? And in the hustle of preparing for Christmas festivities (and last minute shopping), how do you want to keep yourself accountable to focus on enjoying and adoring Jesus?

¹ In those days John the Baptist appeared in the wilderness of Judea, proclaiming, ² "Repent, for the kingdom of heaven has come near." ³ This is the one of whom the prophet Isaiah spoke when he said,

"The voice of one crying out in the wilderness:
'Prepare the way of the Lord,
make his paths straight.' "

⁴ Now John wore clothing of camel's hair with a leather belt around his waist, and his food was locusts and wild honey. ⁵ Then the people of Jerusalem and all Judea were going out to him, and all the region along the Jordan, ⁶ and they were baptized by him in the river Jordan, confessing their sins.

⁷ But when he saw many Pharisees and Sadducees coming for baptism, he said to them, "You brood of vipers! Who warned you to flee from the wrath to come? ⁸ Bear fruit worthy of repentance. ⁹ Do not presume to say to yourselves, 'We have Abraham as our ancestor'; for I tell you, God is able from these stones to raise up children to Abraham. ¹⁰ Even now the ax is lying at the root of the trees; every tree therefore that does not bear good fruit is cut down and thrown into the fire.

¹¹ "I baptize you with water for repentance, but one who is more powerful than I is coming after me; I am not worthy to carry his sandals. He will baptize you with the Holy Spirit and fire. ¹² His winnowing fork is in his hand, and he will clear his threshing floor and will gather his wheat into the granary; but the chaff he will burn with unquenchable fire."

¹³ Then Jesus came from Galilee to John at the Jordan, to be baptized by him. ¹⁴ John would have prevented him, saying, "I need to be baptized by you, and do you come to me?" ¹⁵ But Jesus answered him, "Let it be so now; for it is proper for us in this way to fulfill all righteousness." Then he consented. ¹⁶ And when Jesus had been baptized, just as he came up from the water, suddenly the heavens were opened to him and he saw the Spirit of God descending like a dove and alighting on him. ¹⁷ And a voice from

heaven said, "This is my Son, the Beloved, with whom I am well pleased."

WEEK 4, MONDAY, BIBLE STUDY

READ MATTHEW 3.1–17

HISTORICAL BACKGROUND
Pharisees and Sadducees were among the religious and political powers in ancient Israel. They differed in their philosophy of politics, religious convictions, and theology, and enjoyed different economic power and social class. The Sadducees, who controlled the Temple in Jerusalem, held much more institutional authority. The Pharisees, on the other hand, led a grassroots spiritual renewal among the common people. While their approaches were different, they both aimed to shepherd the Jewish people at the time of Jesus's birth when the nation of Israel was under Roman occupation.

OBSERVATIONS
- How does the author describe John the Baptist?
- What is John's message in this story?
- How does the author describe the response to John's proclamation?

INTERPRETATION
- How would you describe the tone of John's message? Why might you describe it that way?
- How do the people respond to John's message? Why might John's message invite baptisms and confessions?
- Why is repentance connected to the kingdom of heaven's nearness?
- How might the religious leaders have received the words of John?
- What does it mean to bear fruit worthy of repentance? What might that look like in the life of a religious person?

APPLICATION
- In what areas of your life do you need to bear fruit worthy of repentance?
- How might the good news that God is with us and near us (in Jesus), catalyze repentance for you? What do you need to know and believe about Jesus in this season?
- Who are the people in your life who can hear your confession and walk with you in your repentance?

WEEK 4, TUESDAY, IMAGINATIVE READING

READ MATTHEW 3.1–17 SLOWLY ONCE

Reflect on the following questions before reading the passage again.

- What adjectives would you use to describe John the Baptist?
- How does John respond to the success he experiences in his ministry?
- How would you describe John's relationship to the crowd, to the Pharisees and Sadducees, and to Jesus?

As you read the passage a second time, read it from the perspective of John, who obviously knew about the person of Jesus.

- How does knowing Jesus give you perspective on living in repentance?
- How does John express freedom in worship? How might this be in contrast to King Herod who was bound by fear?
- While the passage may be full of pictures of judgment, how do you see John express joy?

John knew Jesus. He knew him not just along familial relationships (they were cousins), but he knew the true identity of Jesus who was sent by God as the Messiah. This knowledge gave John a great amount of freedom to act as a prophetic witness to his community. Knowing the identity of Jesus gives us great joy and freedom to celebrate Jesus as God in the flesh and to live in freedom as called people. Spend some time with God, celebrating him and his Son who has come to dwell among us.

WEEK 4, WEDNESDAY, PSALM 126

We have chosen a psalm that coincides with the week's character and themes. The Psalms have been the prayer book of God's people throughout history. We mature in prayer by regularly spending time in the Psalms, which express the full arc of the human experience to God. Read through the psalm slowly, bringing to mind the story of Herod. Allow the words of the psalmist to become your own prayer.

PSALM 126

A Song of Ascents.

1 When the LORD restored the fortunes of Zion,
   we were like those who dream.
2 Then our mouth was filled with laughter,
   and our tongue with shouts of joy;
   then it was said among the nations,
   "The LORD has done great things for them."
3 The LORD has done great things for us,
   and we rejoiced.
4 Restore our fortunes, O LORD,
   like the watercourses in the Negeb.
5 May those who sow in tears
   reap with shouts of joy.
6 Those who go out weeping,
   bearing the seed for sowing,
   shall come home with shouts of joy,
   carrying their sheaves.

REFLECTION QUESTIONS
- John the Baptist knows the coming of the Messiah means great things for God's people. He also calls his audience to repentance because like the writer of this psalm, he sees the real fractures in humanity.
- What sin, what brokenness do you see in the world today?

- How can you let the psalmist's words guide you in prayer for the light of Jesus to shine on all the darkness you see?
- How do you want to be restored as you wait for Jesus' Second Advent?

WEEK 4, THURSDAY, *LECTIO DIVINA*

Find a place where you will not be distracted. Quiet yourself with some deep breaths. Pray for God—Father, Son, and Holy Spirit—to guide you through this reading.

LECTIO, "READING"

Read Matthew 3.1-17 again. Take your time. Do not focus on anything in particular.

Read the passage again. This time pay attention to a verse or couple of verses that stick out to you.

MEDITATIO, "MEDITATION"

Read that verse several times, slowly and gently.

Are you drawn to a specific word or phrase? Slowly chew on it. Take it in, that is, memorize it. Allow this word to interact with your concerns and desires. Pay attention to what thoughts and feelings this word stirs in you.

ORATIO, "PRAYER"

Ask God, "What are you saying to me through this word?" Listen. Let your meditations shape what you want to say to God.

CONTEMPLATIO, "CONTEMPLATION"

Rest in God's embrace. Let go of your words and be silent. Trust that Jesus fully and deeply loves you. Let the Holy Spirit minister to you.

Take a moment to reflect on your experience praying through this passage. If you use a journal, record your thoughts and prayers there.

WEEK 4, FRIDAY, WRITINGS

Each Friday in this guide, we include writings that further discuss the story and themes of the week. We invite you to ponder the wisdom of these voices that come to us through the centuries. Does something they write stir thoughts or emotions in you? Allow the words of these writers to shape your prayers today.

This voice crying in the wilderness is extraordinary in many ways, but most of all for the single-mindedness with which he pursued his mission even to death, for John the Baptist feared no man, not even Herod the king, and no woman either, not even Herod's wife, who in the end arranged to have his head cut off. But let us take note: this firebrand who recognized no superior was utterly submissive before the One whose coming who lived and died to illuminate. "John said to the people, 'One is coming who is mightier than I, and I am not fit to untie the thong of his sandal'" (Luke 3:15-16). To be the witness, to point away from himself to Jesus Christ—this is the destiny of John, and in these things he is a model for every Christian preacher. — Fleming Rutledge, "A People Prepared"[21]

I had a twenty-three-year-old homie named Miguel working for me on our graffiti crew. As with a great many of our workers, I had met him years earlier while he was detained. He was an extremely nice kid, whose pleasantness was made all the more remarkable by the fact that he had been completely abandoned by his family. Prior to their rejection of him, they had mistreated, abused, and scarred him plenty. He calls me one New Year's Day. "Happy New Year, G."
   "Hey, that's very thoughtful of ya, dog," I say. "You know, Miguel, I was thinkin' of ya—you know, on Christmas. So, whad ya do for Christmas?" I asked knowing that he had no family to welcome him in.

---

[21] Rutledge, "A People Prepared," in *The Bible and The New York Times*, 33.

"Oh, you know, I was just right here," meaning his tiny little apartment, where he lives alone.

"All by yourself?" I ask.

"Oh no," he quickly says, "I invited homies from the crew—you know, *vatos* like me who didn't had no place to go for Christmas."

He names the five homies who came over—all former enemies from rival gangs.

"Really," I tell him, "that sure was nice of you."

But he's got me revved and curious now. "So," I ask him, "what did you do?"

"Well," he says, "you're not gonna believe this ... but ... I cooked a turkey." You can feel his pride right through the phone.

"Wow, you did? Well, how did you prepare it?"

"You know," he says, "Ghetto-style."

I tell him that I'm not really familiar with this recipe.

He's more than happy to give up his secret. "Yeah, well, you just rub it with a gang a' butter, throw a bunch a' salt and pepper on it, squeeze a couple of *limones* over it and put it in the oven. It tasted proper."

I said, "Wow, that's impressive. What else did you have besides the turkey?"

"Just that. Just turkey," he says. His voice tapers to a hush. "Yeah. The six of us, we just sat there, staring at the oven, waiting for the turkey to be done."

One would be hard-pressed to imagine something more sacred and ordinary than these six orphans staring at an oven together. It is the entire law and the prophets, all in one moment, right there, in this humble, holy kitchen.

Not long after this, I give Miguel a ride home after work. I had long been curious about Miguel's own certain resilience. When we arrive at his apartment, I say, "Can I ask you a question? How do you do it? I mean, given all that you've been through—all the pain and stuff you've suffered—how are you like the way you are?"

I genuinely want to know and Miguel has his answer at the ready. "You know, I always suspected that there was something of goodness in me, but I just couldn't find it. Until one day,"—he quiets a bit—"one day, I discovered it here, in my heart. I found it ... goodness. And ever since that day, I have always known who I was." He pauses, caught short by his own truth, (re-teaching loveliness) and turns and looks at me. "And now, nothing can touch me." — Gregory Boyle, *Tattoos on the Heart*[22]

The human race is in a desperate fix. The human race does not need any more spiritual masters; it needs a Savior. The proclamation of John the Baptist is that the one and only Lord of lasting peace and justice is on his way. — Fleming Rutledge, "The Master and the Best Man"[23]

[22] Gregory Boyle, *Tattoos on the Heart: the Power of Boundless Compassion* (New York: Simon and Schuster, Inc., 2010), Kindle Edition, 87-89.
[23] Rutledge, "The Master and the Best Man," in *The Bible and The New York Times*, 41.

WEEK 4, SATURDAY, REFLECTIONS

Take some time today to reflect on how God engaged with you through this devotional this week.

1. Where did you experience the presence of God this week?
2. How has the exposure of the darkness within invite you to embrace the good news that Jesus has come for all sinners?
3. How did the discipline of adoration attune you to the work of God in your life?
4. What are your hopes and prayers for yourself, your community, and your world for the season?

A FINAL WORD

You have now spent four weeks in Matthew's story of Jesus, God incarnate, coming to live among us. As you have seen, it is a story full of wild surprises with a vicious tyrant grasping for power, a virgin giving birth, angels visiting people in their dreams, astrologers from foreign lands arriving to pay homage to a newborn, and a wild prophet calling people to repentance. It is not the story of easy peace. Rather, the incarnation comes as a shock, a bolt of light into a dark world. Some people, like John the Baptist, realign their lives with this new light and others, like Herod, fight against it. Those who submit to God's light find themselves drawn out of their isolation and into community.

As you now celebrate Christmas, take some time to think about your experience of Advent. Consider the following questions. You might answer one or two that stick out to you, or simply let them be a springboard to start your own reflections.

- What in the stories of Herod, Joseph, the wise men, and John the Baptist surprised you the most?
- What are you most thankful for in your time with these stories? What are you least thankful for?
- Was there a method of Bible reading that you found especially life-giving? How might you practice that way of reading more regularly?
- Was there a spiritual discipline that resonated within you? How do you want to incorporate that discipline into your life? With whom do you want to share this discipline?
- In what ways did you see God's growing light through the season of Advent? How do you want to look for this light throughout the year?
- What areas of darkness in the world most concern you? How might you pray for the Holy Spirit to use you to bring the light of the gospel into those spaces?

When Jesus was born, the world changed forever. His incarnation still transforms communities with healing and justice. His light still chases away darkness. As you now enter the season of Christmas, look for signs of Christ's light in the world. Seek ways to participate in bringing this light into all the dark corners of the world.

Let the first stanza of the Christmas carol, "O Holy Night," be for you a closing prayer as you now welcome Jesus, celebrate his presence with us, and hope for his return:

> O holy night! The stars are brightly shining,
> It is the night of our dear Savior's birth.
> Long lay the world in sin and error pining,
> 'Til He appear'd and the soul felt its worth.
> A thrill of hope the weary world rejoices,
> For yonder breaks a new and glorious morn.
> Fall on your knees! O hear the angel voices!
> O night divine, O night when Christ was born;
> O night divine, O night, O night Divine.

BIBLIOGRAPHY

Bonhoeffer, Dietrich. *A Testament to Freedom*. Quoted in *A Year with Dietrich Bonhoeffer: Daily Meditations from His Letters, Writings, and Sermons*. Ed. Carla Barnhill. San Francisco: HarperSanFrancisco, 2005.

Boyle, Gregory. *Tattoos on the Heart: the Power of Boundless Compassion*. New York: Simon and Schuster, Inc., 2010. Kindle Edition.

Calhoun, Adele Ahlberg. *Spiritual Disciplines Handbook: Practices that Transform Us*. Downers Grove, IL: IVP Books, 2005.

Hatina, Thomas R. Hatina. "Exile." In *Dictionary of New Testament Background*. Eds. Craig A. Evans and Stanley E. Porter, 348-351. Downers Grove, IL: InterVarstiy Press, 2000.

Hepper, F. N. "Herbs and Spices." In *New Bible Dictionary*, 3rd ed. Eds. D. R. W. Wood, I. H. Marshall, A. R. Millard, J. I. Packer, and D. J. Wiseman, 465-467. Downers Grove, IL: InterVarsity Press, 1996.

Heschel, Abraham Joshua. "The Spiritual Audacity of Abraham Joshua Heschel." *On Being*. December 6, 2012. http://www.onbeing.org/program/spiritual-audacity-abraham-joshua-heschel/transcript/4951#main_content. Accessed October 24, 2013.

Hoener, Harold W. "Herodian Dynasty." In *Dictionary of Jesus and the Gospels*. Eds. Joel B. Green, Scot McKnight, and I. Howard Marshall, 317-325. Downers Grove, IL: InterVarsity Press, 1992.

Keener, Craig S. *The IVP Bible Background Commentary: New Testament*. Downers Grove, IL: InterVarsity Press, 1993. Electronic Edition.

King, Martin Luther, Jr. "Our God is Able." In *Strength to Love*. Philadelphia: Fortress Press, 1963.

Matthew 1-13. Ancient Christian Commentary on Scripture, New Testament 1a. Ed. Manilo Simonetti. Downers Grove, IL: InterVarsity Press, 2001.

Nouwen, Henri J. M. *The Way of the Heart: The Spirituality of the Desert Fathers and Mothers*. New York: HarperCollins, 1981.

Rutledge, Fleming. "Advent Begins in the Dark." In *The Bible and The New York Times*. Grand Rapids, MI: Eerdmans Publishing Company, 1998.

------. "A People Prepared." In *The Bible and The New York Times*.

------. "The Master and the Best Man." In *The Bible and The New York Times*.

Witherington, Ben, III. "Birth of Jesus." In *Dictionary of Jesus and the Gospels*. 60-74.

Wright , J. S. and J. A. Thompson. "Marriage." In *New Bible Dictionary*, 3rd ed. 732-736.

ABOUT THE AUTHORS

Eddy Ekmekji was born in Baghdad, Iraq, to Armenian parents, spent a part of his childhood in Beirut Lebanon, and immigrated to the United States (California) in 1986 at the age of 10. In high school, he came to deeper faith at his local church that motivated him to continue to grow in his own discipleship. He went to college at UC Davis, where he got involved and eventually joined the staff team of InterVarsity Christian Fellowship. Since 1998, he's been serving on college campuses as a campus minister. He and his wife and three children live in Los Angeles where he directs the ministry to Black Students. He received his Master of Arts from Fuller Theological Seminary. He blogs at Serving Bread (servingbread.com).

Tyler Watson is a native Californian. He is a stay-at-home dad living in the Bay Area of northern California with his wife and son. Prior to his current vocation he served as a pastor in congregations of the Evangelical Covenant Church. He received his Master of Divinity from Fuller Theological Seminary. He blogs at The Space Between My Ears (spacebetweenmyears.com).

Eddy and Tyler became friends as students at UC Davis in 1998, where they learned to follow God, ministered together, and traveled to China as part of a cultural-language exchange program. They remain good friends.

Eddy is also the author of:
Knowing God's Word
Because God is Great: An Effective Model for Christian Living and Maturity

Tyler is also the author of:
Delivered from All My Fears: Devotional Readings on Psalm 34
My Companions are in Darkness: Devotional Readings on Psalm 88
On the Glorious Splendor: Devotional Readings on Psalm 145

5977226R00049

Made in the USA
San Bernardino, CA
27 November 2013